Alien Adventures

Cat's Picnic

Alison Hawes ● Jonatronix

T0351656

OXFORD
UNIVERSITY PRESS

In this story ...

Cat

Nok

duck

Mum

Cat's sister

picnic bag

zip

box

bun

rug

3

buzz

Cat unzips the bag.

Nok is in the box!

A duck pecks at the picnic.

The duck picks up Nok.

Cat yells.

Nok drops the bun.

The duck picks up the bun.

Nok is stuck in the mud.

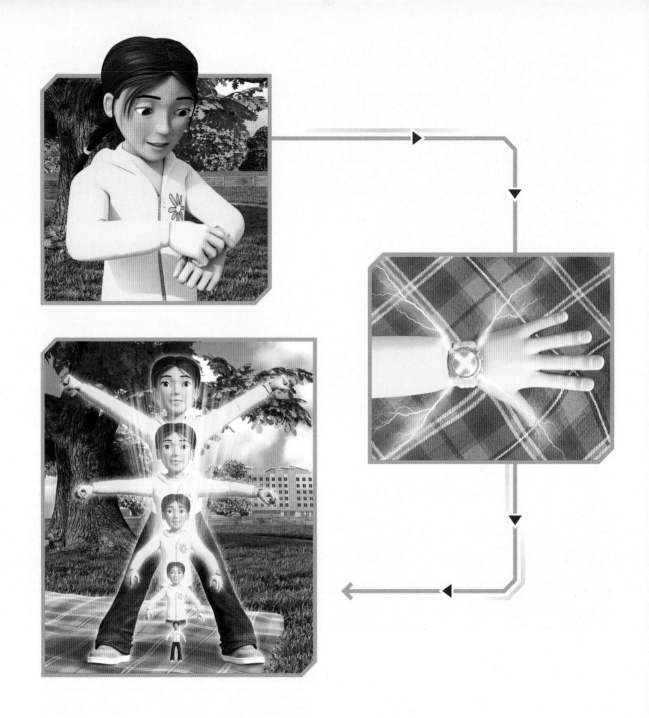

Cat presses the X.

twig

She has to cross the mud.

Cat gets Nok.

Cat and Nok tuck into the picnic.

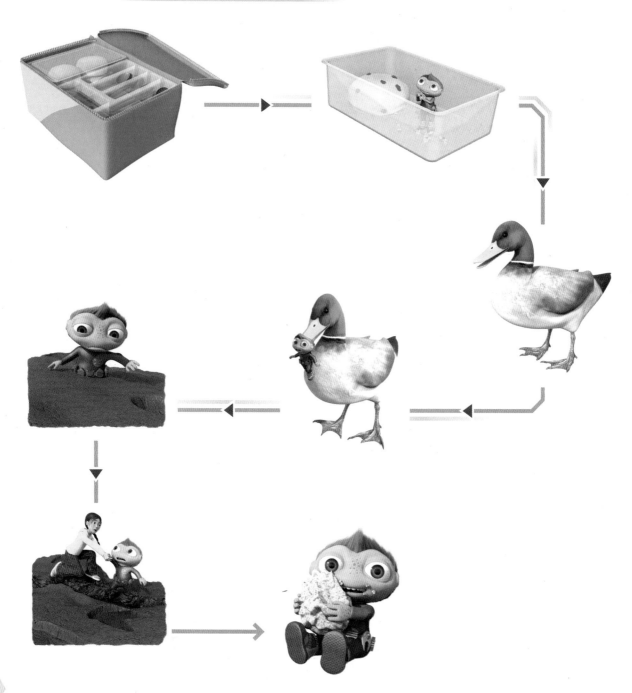